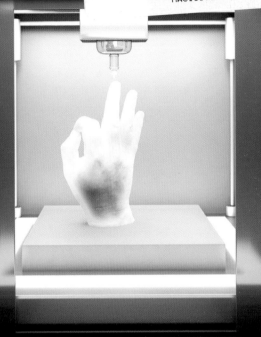

3D
PRINTING

JOHN PERRITANO

red rhino
b**OO**k s®
NONFICTION

3D Printing	Medal of Honor
Area 51	Monsters of the Deep
Bioweapons	Monsters on Land
Cannibal Animals	The Science of Movies
Cloning	Seven Wonders of the
Comet Catcher	Ancient World
Drones	Tuskegee Airmen
Fault Lines	Virtual Reality
Gnarly Sports Injuries	Wild Weather
Great Spies of the World	Witchcraft
Hacked	Wormholes
Little Rock Nine	

Photo credits: page 11: evan Hurd / Alamy.com; page 14: 3D Systems / 3dsystems.com; page 30: travelview / shutterstock.com; page 31: Tinxi / shutterstock.com; pages 36-37: Tinxi / shutterstock.com;

SADDLEBACK
EDUCATIONAL PUBLISHING
www.sdlback.com

ISBN-13: 978-1-68021-073-6
ISBN-10: 1-68021-073-4
eBook: 978-1-63078-375-4

Printed in Malaysia

22 21 20 19 18   1 2 3 4 5

TABLE OF CONTENTS

Chapter 1
SAVING THE DAY

Ben is a runner.
He puts on shoes.
Then he pulls his laces tight.
One snaps.

Oh no!
He needs a new lace.
There is no time.
The race is soon.
His team needs him.

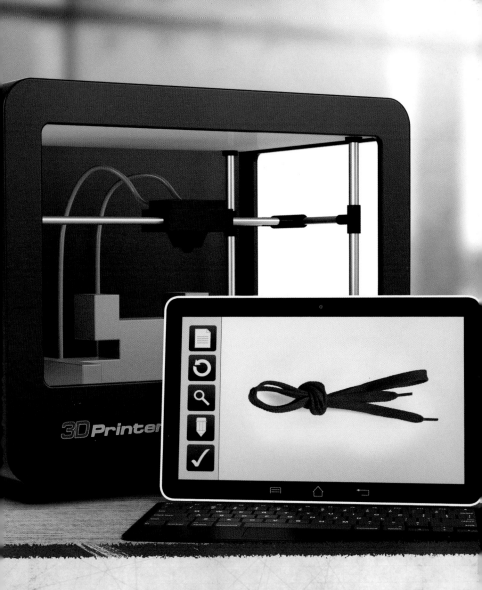

Ben opens his laptop.

He searches.

There is a *plan*.

It is for a new lace.

He copies it.

Ben picks the color.
It is red.
That is the team color.
He goes to the printer.
It starts to hum.
Then it stops.

Ben grabs the lace.

He strings it.

Then he ties his shoe.

A printer saved the day.

It was a *3D printer*.

Chapter 2

WHAT IS 3D PRINTING?

Many printers use ink.

3D printers do not.

Some use wax.

Others use *plastic*.

Metal can be used too.

3D printers make many things.

These can be toys or car parts.

They can even make bones and pizza.

Think about this book.

There are words on the page.

They are made from ink.

The ink sits on paper.

There are two *layers*.

Paper is one.

Ink is the other.

3D-printed
car parts

7

Material for 3D printing

3D printers are different.
They print a layer.
Another layer is added.
This keeps going.
It can happen millions of times.

The layers build.
An object takes shape.
Finally it is ready to use.

Chapter 3

HOW DID IT START?

3D printing is not new.
It started in the 1980s.
Many worked on it.

It was 1984.
A man filed a *patent*.
His name is Chuck Hull.
He lives in the US.

Hull had made a printer.
It made *prototypes*.
These are *models*.
Many companies use them.

Hull's 3D company was founded in California.

Chuck Hull was
inducted into the
National Inventors
Hall of Fame in 2014.

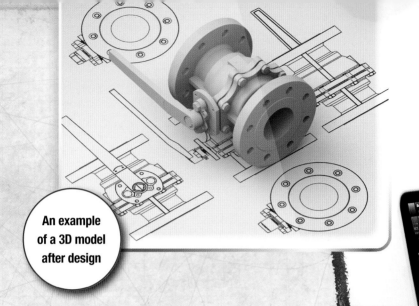

An example of a 3D model after design

Let's say a company has an idea.
They want to make a new product.
First they have to see if it works.
They make a model.
Is it the right size and shape?
Design is tested too.
Is it easy to use?
Can it be made better?

The company finds out.
Then they make the real thing.
But models cost a lot.
Making them takes time.

1980s

Hull's printer was faster.

Models still cost a lot.

But the printer made them cheaper.

TODAY

Today's printers have come a long way.
They are much more powerful.
Many things are possible.

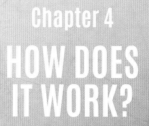

Chapter 4

HOW DOES IT WORK?

3D printing is not hard.

Many people do it.

A plan is needed.

It tells the printer what to do.

Some make their own plans.

They use *software*.

Others find a plan online.

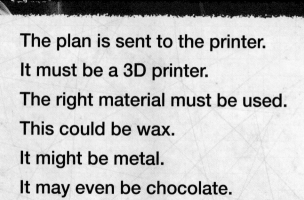

The plan is sent to the printer.

It must be a 3D printer.

The right material must be used.

This could be wax.

It might be metal.

It may even be chocolate.

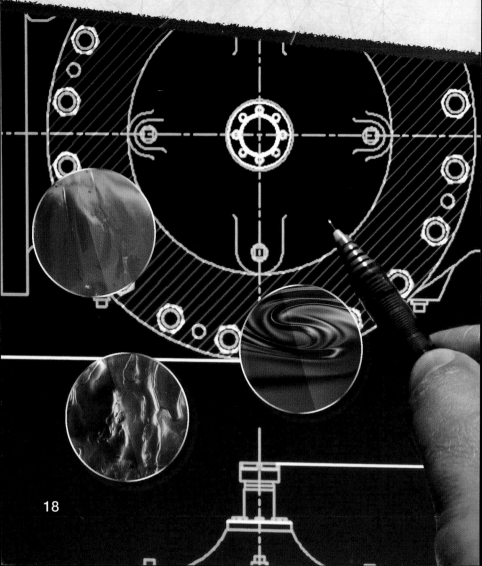

The printer melts the material.

Then it builds layers.

It follows the plan.

The material gets hard.

More layers are added.

Then it is done.

Liquid dough can be used in 3D printing.

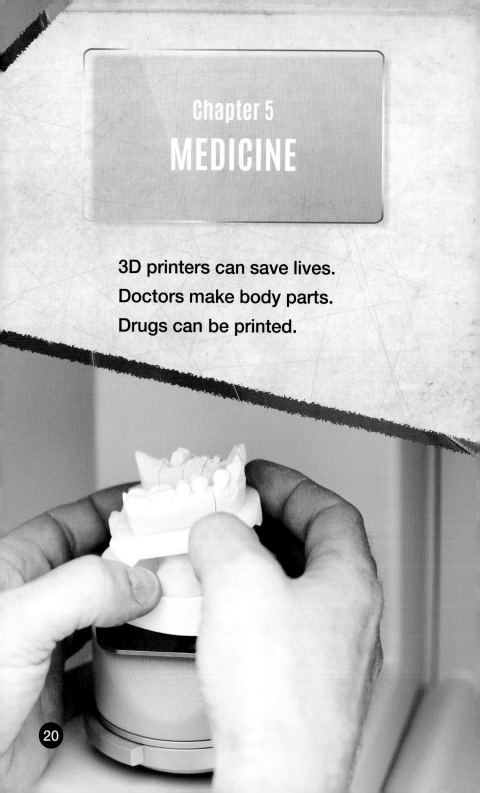

Chapter 5
MEDICINE

3D printers can save lives.
Doctors make body parts.
Drugs can be printed.

It was 2015.
A drug was okayed.
It had been printed.
This was a first.

The drug helps the sick.
Each pill is custom-made.
The *dose* is exactly right.
The pills are smooth.
They are easy to swallow.

3D printers make tools.

One studies breath.

It tests for *diseases*.

Cancers can be found.

Other diseases can too.

The tool is cheap.

Other tests cost more.

This saves money.

Body parts can be printed.

Ears are easy.

Noses are too.

They are mostly soft tissue.

It is called *cartilage*.

Other body parts are harder to print.

Not all can be made yet.

3D

A 3D World

Researchers in Spain
have developed a
printer that will
print human skin.

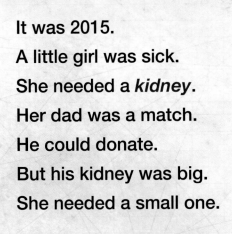

It was 2015.

A little girl was sick.

She needed a *kidney*.

Her dad was a match.

He could donate.

But his kidney was big.

She needed a small one.

A 3D printer was used.

It made models.

The first was the girl's belly.

The second was the dad's kidney.

It was a big kidney.

How would it fit the girl?

Doctors planned.

They got ready for the *operation*.

The model helped.

It made the operation safer.

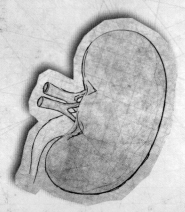

A close-up of cancer cells

It was 2015.

A man was sick.

He had cancer.

Doctors made a decision.

He needed new ribs.

A printer made them.

It used *titanium*.

That is a metal.

The new ribs worked.

Chapter 6
FOOD

3D printers have other uses.
Food can be printed.
It is made layer by layer.
Some say it tastes good.

How does it work?
Cartridges have frozen food inside.
These go in the printer.

It can make a pizza.
There are layers.
First there is the crust.
Then sauce is added.
Cheese goes on top.
This process is fast.
Then it is ready for the oven.

NASA paid for a *study*.

They wanted to cook in space.

Food in space is *freeze-dried*.

It lasts for a long time.

But it is not very tasty.

Some get tired of it.

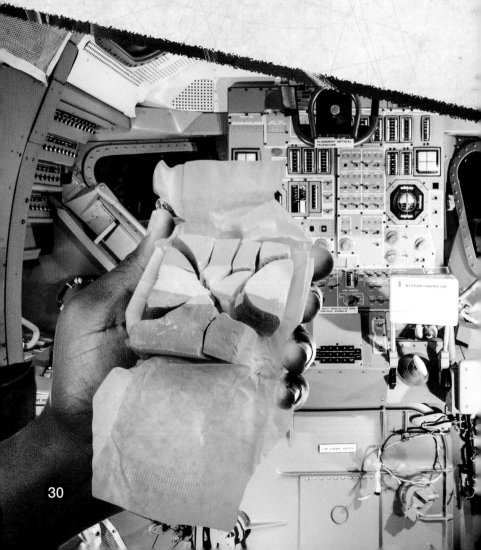

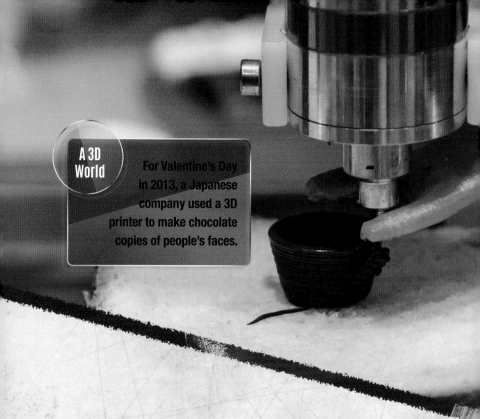

3D printing changes that.
Many foods can be made.
The food tastes good.
It is healthy.
Cooking is fast.

Some restaurants are doing this.
Theme parks are too.
Chefs can be creative.
They can try new things.
Many want to eat this food.

The military has plans.

It wants to print food.

This could be used on the battlefield.

It would save money.

There would be less waste.

They would print only what is needed.

There is less packaging.

It gets rid of food rot.

Printing food could help the hungry.

These printers are changing the world.

Chapter 7
FASHION

3D printers are changing fashion.
Jewelry can be hard to make.
There are many steps.
It can take a long time.
Tools are used.
The metal is heated.
Then it is shaped.
A printer changes this.
The process is fast.
It is simple too.

People make designs.
Some print with silver.
Others use gold.
There are other metals too.
The printer melts the metal.
Then it prints the design.
Gems are added later.

DESKTOP 3D PRINTER

Clothing can be printed too.
Some pieces are made with plastic.
Others are made with *Filaflex*.
It is a kind of plastic.
But it is flexible.
It stretches and bends.

Shoes can be printed.
Feet can be hard to fit.
A person's feet are not the same.
One foot might be one size.
The other could be bigger.
Widths can vary too.
3D printing solves this.
Printers make the exact size.

A 3D-printed shoe

A 3D World

3D fashions have been worn on the red carpet and fashion runways.

Chapter 8
POLICE

Police use 3D printers.
Something bad happens.
There has been a crime.
It can be hard to figure out.
A model can help.

Lasers are used.
They scan the scene.
Then the printer makes a model.
The model can be big.
It shows the scene.
Police solve the crime.

A 3D World

Police are using 3D printers to make models of shoes that fit over footprints. This helps identify the type of shoe they are looking for.

Models can be used in court.
Juries can see a crime scene.
This helps them.
They see where it happened.
It makes more sense.

40

Phones can be locked.
Some phones use fingerprints.
These unlock them.

Let's say police have a phone.
They need to unlock it.
3D printers are used.
They take a fingerprint.
A model is made.
The phone unlocks.

There are other uses.
Cold cases are old.
These have not been solved.
The victim is not known.
But there might be a skull.
This is used to make a plan.
The printer makes a model.
It is shared.
People see it.
It might be on the news.
Someone may know the person.
This helps solve the crime.

Chapter 9
CRIME

Not all uses are good.

It was 2013.

A boy wanted to make a gun.

He found a plan.

It was online.

He copied it.

Then he printed it.

The gun was plastic.

But it could shoot.

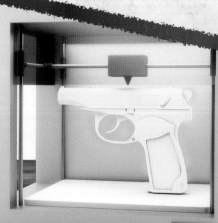

Criminals print fakes.

Some make watches.

Others make purses.

They look real.

But they are not.

Some print labels.

They have a purse.

Then a label is added.

They sell it.

Buyers pay a lot.

They are getting ripped off.

Others have printed fake ATMs.

These look like ATMs.

But they are not.

People want cash.

Their card goes in.

It does not work.

But a machine reads it.

The numbers are saved.

Criminals use them.

They buy things.

The card owner gets the bill.

There will be new crimes.

But police are keeping track.

They will stop them.

Chapter 10
WHAT'S NEXT?

3D printing brings changes.
Food is changing.
People are printing food.
It may be eaten in space.
It could feed soldiers too.
Could this help the hungry?

3D printers solve crimes.
They cause some too.
Will laws be passed to help with this?

The way things are made is changing.
Some have been hard to make.
3D printers make it easy.
Models are cheaper.
Companies can try more ideas.

There might be a bigger change.
Shopping may change.
Businesses will have less control.
People will have more.
They can make things at home.
Printing is fast.
Costs are low.
There may be less need for stores.

Printing has changed.
Our world will change with it.
What will the future hold?
There are no limits.

GLOSSARY

3D printer: a machine that makes objects by laying down thin layers over and over until the object is finished

cartilage: a strong but flexible material found in some parts of the body

cartridge: a container that goes into a machine

cold case: a criminal investigation that has not been solved for a long time

design: the way something has been made

disease: an illness that harms the body

dose: an amount of medicine

Filaflex: a type of flexible plastic that can be used in 3D printers to make clothing

freeze-dried: food that has been preserved by freezing and drying it

kidney: a body part that gets rid of waste in the blood

layer: an amount of something that is spread over an area; some things have many layers

model: a copy of something that is tested before making the real thing

operation: a surgical procedure

patent: a document that recognizes someone as the inventor and owner of something

plan: a set of steps to make something

plastic: a light, strong material

prototype: a first model of something that is used to show how copies should be made

software: a program that runs on a computer

study: an organized plan where many things are looked at to learn more about something

titanium: a very strong metal

VIRTUAL REALITY

Many companies have hologram devices.
Sony makes one.
Put it on.
Shine light on a cartoon robot.
The robot will close its eyes.

Microsoft has a tinted *visor*.
It puts holograms on top of
the real world.
A VR glass on a real table.
A VR monster in your bedroom.
Fantasies become real.
You can use it for work.
Or for fun.

THAT'S COOL
Scientists want to use a
hologram visor to explore
Mars.

36

37

How does this work?
HMDs have two screens.
One for each eye.
This tricks a person's eyes.
They think they are seeing things for real.
But it's all virtual.

VR has taken off since then.
People are testing new tools.
Joysticks.
A *mouse*.
Even gloves.

Chapter 2
THE SOMETIMES REAL WORLD

Virtual reality.
VR for short.
It seems real.
But it is created by computers.
Why does it seem real?
It has three *dimensions*.

Height.
Width.
Depth.
Just like the real world.

You can play in the virtual world.
Work.
Take trips.
Meet new people.
You can try new things.
Fly a jet.
Race a car.
Walk on Mars.
Hold a person's heart in your hand.

red rhino b👓👓ks®

NONFICTION

9781680210736

9781680210316

9781680210729

9781680210484

9781680210347

9781680210477

9781680210293

9781680210538

9781680210712

9781680210491

9781680210378

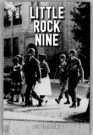
9781680210552

WWW.REDRHINOBOOKS.COM

9781680210545

9781680210286

9781680210309

9781680210507

9781680210354

9781680210521

9781680210361

9781680210514

9781680210323

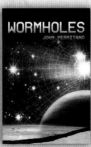
9781680210330

MORE
TITLES
COMING
SOON